D1524550

CH▲NGE
HAS
CH▶NGED

TIME FOR A STRATEGIC RESET

STUDY GUIDE

Copyright © 2021 by Samuel R. Chand

Published by AVAIL

All rights reserved. No portion of this book may be reproduced, stored in a retrieval system, or transmitted in any form or by any means—electronic, mechanical, photocopy, recording, scanning, or other—except for brief quotations in critical reviews or articles, without prior written permission of the author.

All scripture is taken from the Holy Bible, New International Version®, NIV®. Copyright © 1973, 1978, 1984, 2011 by Biblica, Inc.™ Used by permission of Zondervan. All rights reserved worldwide. www.zondervan.com. The "NIV" and "New International Version" are trademarks registered in the United States Patent and Trademark Office by Biblica, Inc.™

For foreign and subsidiary rights, contact the author.

Cover design: Whitaker House

CH▲NGE
HAS
CH▲NGED

TIME FOR A STRATEGIC RESET

STUDY GUIDE

SAM CHAND

AVAIL

CONTENTS

NEVER THE SAME AGAIN

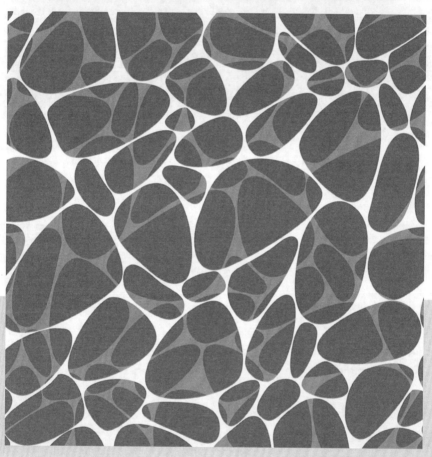

*"Too much has changed for us to go back
to the way things used to be. In fact, the
very nature of change has changed!"*

As you read
Chapter 1:
"Never the
Same Again"
in *Change
Has Changed*,
review, reflect
on, and respond
to the text by
answering
the following
questions.

REVIEW, REFLECT, AND RESPOND:

What does change mean to you? Define it in your own words.

_____

_____

_____

_____

_____

What has been the biggest change you or your organization has undergone in recent years?

_____

_____

_____

_____

_____

In your opinion, how has society changed over the past year? What key events sparked this/these change(s)?

_____

_____

_____

_____

_____

_____

What do you think the following verse from 2 Thessalonians reveals about our effectiveness and fruition through God? Does this apply to just us, or our organizations as well?

_____

_____

_____

_____

_____

_____

_____

_____

_____

> *With this in mind, we constantly pray for you, that our God may make you worthy of his calling, and that by his power he may bring to fruition your every desire for goodness and your every deed prompted by faith.*
>
> *—2 Thessalonians 1:11*

How can adaptation and change help us to see who's performing well and who's not within our organizations?

_____

_____

_____

_____

_____

_____

_____

Of the societal shifts, dilemmas, and divides discussed in this chapter, which do you think has been the most impactful and why?

_____

_____

_____

_____

_____

_____

_____

_____

_____

Why do you think flexibility is important in times like these?

_____

_____

_____

_____

_____

_____

_____

_____

_____

_____

What leadership changes have you made to accommodate organizational and cultural change?

_____

_____

_____

_____

_____

_____

_____

_____

_____

What is a change agent? Are all leaders automatically change agents by definition?

_____

_____

_____

_____

_____

_____

_____

_____

_____

_____

_____

_____

CHAPTER 2

THREE MASSIVE SHIFTS

"No matter where and who you lead, you're in the middle of a society-changing inflection point."

12 | THREE MASSIVE SHIFTS

As you read Chapter 2: "Three Massive Shifts" in *Change Has Changed*, review, reflect on, and respond to the text by answering the following questions.

REVIEW, REFLECT, AND RESPOND:

What shifts has your organization experienced recently? Explain at least one in detail.

_____

_____

_____

_____

_____

_____

_____

_____

_____

How did the pandemic affect your organization's operations?

_____

_____

_____

_____

_____

_____

_____

_____

_____

_____

_____

_____

Do you feel you adapted effectively to the change that has been occurring? Why or why not?

_____

_____

_____

_____

_____

> *And we know that in all things God works for the good of those who love him, who have been called according to his purpose.*
>
> *—Romans 8:28*

Why is this verse from Romans 8 important to remember in the midst of change?

_____

_____

_____

_____

_____

How can isolation be an enemy of change? What's the danger?

_____

_____

_____

_____

_____

_____

Does the current society shift only affect some
leaders and not others?

_____

_____

_____

_____

_____

_____

_____

_____

_____

How can crises be advantageous to us in
determining who are key players within our
organizations?

_____

_____

_____

_____

_____

_____

_____

_____

_____

_____

Of the three major shifts discussed in this chapter, which do you feel you've been the most effective in adapting to? Why?

_____

_____

_____

_____

_____

_____

_____

_____

_____

_____

Which of the three shifts do you feel you've been least effective in adapting to? Why?

_____

_____

_____

_____

_____

_____

_____

_____

_____

_____

THE PACE OF CHANGE

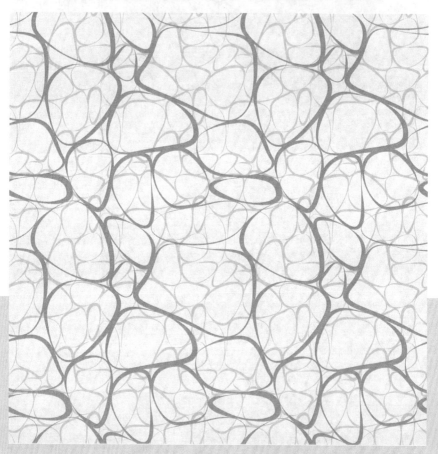

"More than ever, leaders have to think and act on the fly to communicate with clarity, confidence, and kindness to every person associated with the organization."

As you read Chapter 3: "The Pace of Change" in *Change Has Changed*, review, reflect on, and respond to the text by answering the following questions.

REVIEW, REFLECT, AND RESPOND:

In your experience, has organizational change happened fast or slow? Has it ever been difficult to manage due to the speed of change?

_____

_____

_____

_____

_____

_____

_____

_____

_____

_____

What do you think happens to an organization if the leader can't keep up with the pace of change?

_____

_____

_____

_____

_____

_____

_____

_____

_____

_____

_____

Do you think there are any organizations, fields, or areas that don't need to worry about change? If so, what are they?

_____

_____

_____

_____

_____

> *Therefore go and make disciples of all nations, baptizing them in the name of the Father and the Son and the Holy Spirit, and teaching them to obey everything I have commanded you. And surely I am with you always, to the very end of the age.*
>
> *—Matthew 28:19-20*

Why is it important to remember the closing of Matthew 28:19-20, "…I am with you always, to the very end of the age?"

_____

_____

_____

_____

_____

What happens if we put off all our decision-making until we have 100% of the needed information?

_____

_____

_____

_____

_____

_____

Why do leaders need to be intentional about clarifying during seasons of rapid change?

_____

_____

_____

_____

_____

_____

_____

_____

_____

Have the decisions you've made as a leader ever faced opposition? Did this discourage you?

_____

_____

_____

_____

_____

_____

_____

_____

_____

_____

_____

How has your decision-making changed in the past year? Do you think this is a healthy change?

_____

_____

_____

_____

_____

_____

_____

_____

_____

_____

Is speed the only important factor in decision-making amidst change? Should we focus on anything else?

_____

_____

_____

_____

_____

_____

_____

_____

_____

_____

_____

CHAPTER 4

PEOPLE OF CHANGE

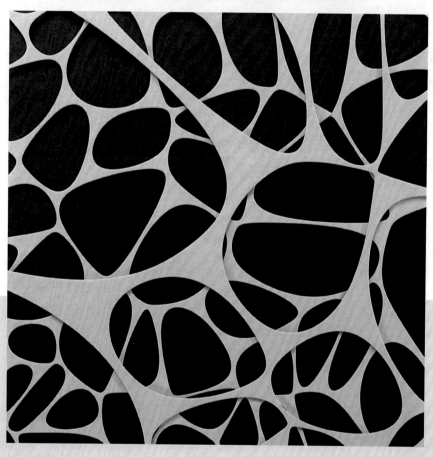

*"A crisis doesn't create character and talent,
but it reveals what's always been there."*

As you read
Chapter 4:
"People of
Change" in
*Change Has
Changed*,
review, reflect
on, and respond
to the text by
answering
the following
questions.

REVIEW, REFLECT, AND RESPOND:

Have the recent societal shifts caused a
change to your organizational chart? If so,
how has it changed?

_____

_____

_____

_____

_____

_____

_____

_____

_____

Have you noticed anyone you lead step up
more than others during crises? Why do you
think this is important to take note of?

_____

_____

_____

_____

_____

_____

_____

_____

_____

_____

_____

How do you think spirits of uncertainty and anxiety take root in an organization? How can a leader prevent this?

_____

_____

_____

_____

_____

_____

_____

_____

> *Do not be anxious about anything, but in every situation, by prayer and petition, with thanksgiving, present your requests to God.*
>
> *—Philippians 4:6*

What does Philippians 4:6 reveal about anxiety and how we should treat it?

_____

_____

_____

_____

_____

_____

_____

_____

How can change in an organizational chart change the output of an organization?

_____

_____

_____

_____

_____

_____

_____

_____

_____

_____

Do you think a deep and true care for the wellbeing of others translates to effective leadership?

_____

_____

_____

_____

_____

_____

_____

_____

_____

_____

What does empathy look like in leadership? Are you an empathetic leader?

_____

_____

_____

_____

_____

_____

_____

Of the strategies discussed to avoid the many distractions life brings, which do you most need to work on?

_____

_____

_____

_____

_____

_____

_____

How can lack of empathy hurt not only our leadership and those we lead but also our organization?

_____

_____

_____

_____

_____

_____

THE PROCESS OF CHANGE

"*In times of crisis, the effects of change are multiplied because rapid changes are happening both outside and inside the organization.*"

As you read Chapter 5: "The Process of Change" in *Change Has Changed*, review, reflect on, and respond to the text by answering the following questions.

REVIEW, REFLECT, AND RESPOND:

How can an improper perspective of change affect our ability to navigate it effectively?

_____

_____

_____

_____

_____

_____

_____

_____

_____

_____

Do you think reevaluating at regular intervals is important when implementing change?

_____

_____

_____

_____

_____

_____

_____

_____

_____

Does uncertainty stop you and your organization from functioning? If not, why?

_____

_____

_____

_____

_____

_____

_____

_____

> *"Suppose one of you wants to build a tower. Won't you first sit down and estimate the cost to see if you have enough money to complete it?"*
>
> *—Luke 14:28*

This verse from Luke 14 speaks to the importance of estimation and planning—do you think this applies to our organizations as well?

_____

_____

_____

_____

_____

_____

_____

What are some of the advantages of reevaluating our change plan?

_____

_____

_____

_____

_____

_____

_____

_____

_____

_____

_____

How can external crises increase the change we're seeing within the organization?

_____

_____

_____

_____

_____

_____

_____

_____

_____

_____

_____

_____

What happens to an organization and its operations if leaders aren't honest in introspection and reevaluation?

_____

_____

_____

_____

_____

What does it mean to "tolerate ambiguity?" Would those you lead say you tolerate ambiguity?

_____

_____

_____

_____

_____

_____

How can our perception and attention to change make or break our organizations?

_____

_____

_____

_____

_____

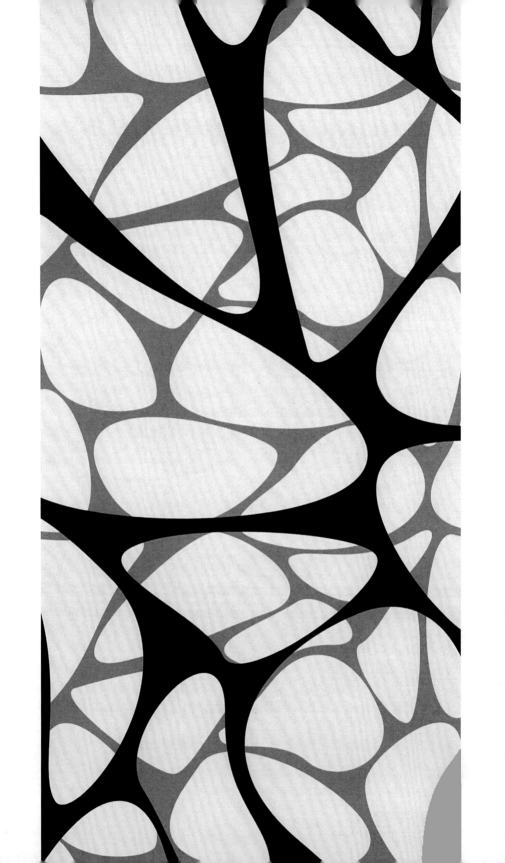

PROGRAMS IN CHANGE

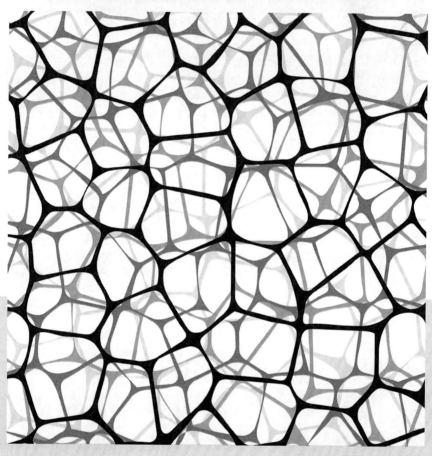

"Use a pencil with a good eraser because the one thing we can be certain about is uncertainty."

As you read Chapter 6: "Programs in Change" in *Change Has Changed*, review, reflect on, and respond to the text by answering the following questions.

REVIEW, REFLECT, AND RESPOND:

What changes have your organization's programs experienced in the last year?

_____

_____

_____

_____

_____

_____

_____

_____

_____

What event or dilemma caused you to make the above changes? Were the program changes successful in addressing the issue?

_____

_____

_____

_____

_____

_____

_____

_____

_____

_____

Are there any programs in your organization right now that you think need drastic changes? Why?

_____

_____

_____

_____

_____

_____

_____

_____

_____

> *I know what it is to be in need, and I know what it is to have plenty. I have learned the secret of being content in any and every situation, whether well fed or hungry, whether living in plenty or in want. I can do all things through him who gives me strength.*
>
> *—Philippians 4:12-13*

In this verse, Paul speaks of his ability to be content in any situation. How is this possible?

_____

_____

_____

_____

_____

_____

How can data actually be harmful to our ability to connect with people?

_____

_____

_____

_____

_____

_____

_____

_____

What are the advantages of data? How can we make sure we're using it effectively?

_____

_____

_____

_____

_____

_____

_____

_____

_____

_____

_____

_____

What does it mean to "elevate the innovators?" Who is an innovator in your organization?

_____

_____

_____

_____

_____

_____

_____

How can a realistic view of uncertainty make us more flexible and effective in the long run?

_____

_____

_____

_____

_____

_____

Why are feedback loops important when implementing new systems?

_____

_____

_____

_____

_____

_____

PROCLAMATION IN CHANGE

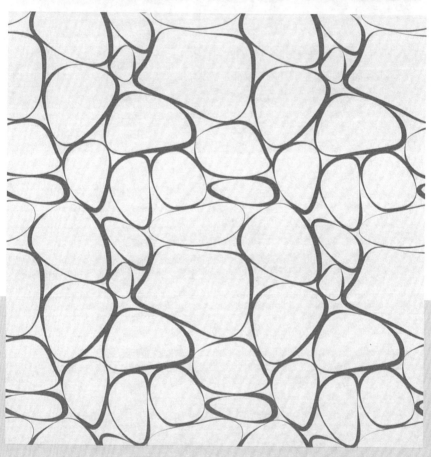

"If you connect with them emotionally, they'll be more willing and able to hear your reasoning."

As you read
Chapter 7:
"Proclamation
in Change"
in *Change
Has Changed*,
review, reflect
on, and respond
to the text by
answering
the following
questions.

REVIEW, REFLECT, AND RESPOND:

Define what effective communication from a leader looks and sounds like to you. Are you an effective communicator by this standard?

_____

_____

_____

_____

_____

_____

_____

_____

_____

_____

What area of your communication do you need to improve in?

_____

_____

_____

_____

_____

_____

_____

_____

How do you and your team connect? What brings your organization together?

_____

_____

_____

_____

_____

_____

_____

_____

> *For we do not have a high priest who is unable to empathize with our weaknesses, but we have one who has been tempted in every way, just as we are—yet he did not sin.*
>
> *—Hebrews 4:15*

What does this verse in Hebrews reveal about Christ's ability to empathize with our weaknesses? Do you think this is an important trait for leaders to possess?

_____

_____

_____

_____

_____

_____

_____

How do you encourage those you lead? How does this affect their output?

_____

_____

_____

_____

_____

_____

_____

_____

_____

_____

Why is the ability to connect on an emotional and personal level so important?

_____

_____

_____

_____

_____

_____

_____

_____

_____

Do you think it's possible to overcommunicate? Why or why not?

_____

_____

_____

_____

_____

_____

_____

Which is more important: rational communication or emotional communication?

_____

_____

_____

_____

_____

_____

_____

Why are communication plans so essential as your organization grows?

_____

_____

_____

_____

_____

_____

_____

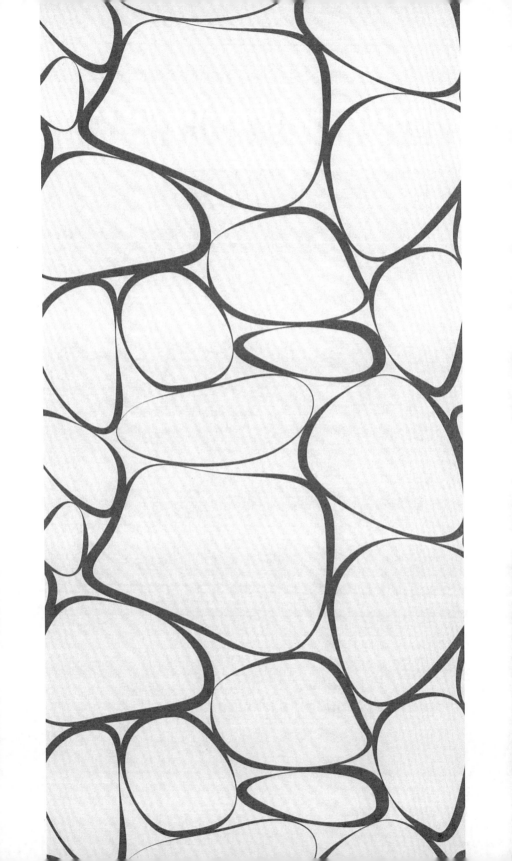

CHAPTER 8

PREPARATION FOR CHANGE

*"Preparations are broad and strategic;
planning is narrow and tactical."*

REVIEW, REFLECT, AND RESPOND:

In your own words, what does it mean to prepare for change? Is this a physical preparation or a mental preparation?

_____

_____

_____

_____

_____

_____

_____

_____

_____

_____

_____

_____

What is the difference between preparation and planning?

_____

_____

_____

_____

_____

_____

_____

_____

How can an organization's culture be prepared for change? Is this an easy process?

_____

_____

_____

_____

_____

_____

_____

> *Jesus Christ is the same yesterday and today and forever.*
>
> *—Hebrews 13:8*

Why is this verse from Hebrews 13 so important to remember amidst preparing for change?

_____

_____

_____

_____

_____

What does it mean to 'continually prepare?' Is your organization practicing this currently?

_____

_____

_____

_____

_____

How do we ensure our organizations are agile? What's our starting point?

_____

_____

_____

_____

_____

_____

_____

_____

_____

Are you intentional about planning for your organization's longevity? Why or why not?

_____

_____

_____

_____

_____

_____

_____

_____

_____

_____

Does your organization suffer from 'change battle fatigue?' If so, what can you do to combat it?

_____

_____

_____

_____

_____

_____

_____

_____

What are the changes that your organization is ready to tackle? How can you as the leader get it more prepared?

_____

_____

_____

_____

_____

_____

_____

_____

_____

_____

PERSONAL CARE IN CHANGING TIMES

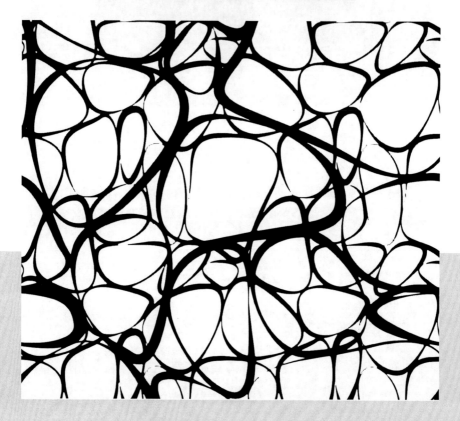

"In the crush of having to make snap decisions—and experiencing both internal doubts and external pushback—it's important to stay closely connected to the only true source of stability, wisdom, and joy."

As you read
Chapter 9:
"Personal Care
in Changing
Times" in
*Change Has
Changed*,
review, reflect
on, and respond
to the text by
answering
the following
questions.

REVIEW, REFLECT, AND RESPOND:

Do you think it's important for leaders to invest in themselves—not just in their personal growth, but their personal wellbeing? Explain.

_____

_____

_____

_____

_____

_____

_____

_____

_____

Have you ever questioned your capacity to lead? If so, explain the situation and the mindset you had at the time.

_____

_____

_____

_____

_____

_____

_____

_____

_____

_____

> *Rejoice with those who rejoice; mourn with those who mourn.*
>
> —*Romans 12:15*

Who do you have in your life that mourns when you mourn and rejoices when you rejoice, as is spoken of in Romans 12:15?

_____

_____

_____

_____

_____

_____

_____

_____

Of the different leadership pressures discussed, which have you struggled with most?

_____

_____

_____

_____

_____

_____

_____

_____

What do you do to recharge? How often do you do it?

_____

_____

_____

_____

_____

_____

_____

_____

_____

_____

Why is our spiritual health so important as leaders, even if we aren't leading in a ministry setting?

_____

_____

_____

_____

_____

_____

_____

_____

_____

_____

Who do you have in your life that you can call a true friend? Why are friends so important to our longevity as leaders?

_____

_____

_____

_____

_____

_____

_____

_____

_____

How can friends become our 'cities of refuge?' What does this mean?

_____

_____

_____

_____

_____

_____

_____

_____

_____

_____